GROWING UP ON THE CARNIVAL

Terry Brodbeck Ward

Knotted Road Press
www.KnottedRoadPress.com

Growing Up on the Carnival
Copyright © 2014 by Terry Brodbeck Ward
All rights reserved
Published 2014 by Knotted Road Press
Cover and interior design copyright © 2014 by Knotted Road Press
www.KnottedRoadPress.com

ISBN: 978-0692303405

This book is licensed for your personal enjoyment only. All rights reserved.
This book, or parts thereof, may not be reproduced in any form without permission.

This book is dedicated to
Leah, who made it all possible
Ken, who helped with research
Brian, who inspired the work

Figure 1: Charles Brodbeck

When I was growing up, I thought all children spent their childhood living on a carnival. It wasn't until I was taking an English class in college that I realized my early years were unique.

Charles Brodbeck, my great-grandfather, was born in Marseilles, Illinois, in 1857. He came to western Kansas to homestead his six hundred and forty acres (a section of land) in the 1890s. He began farming in Keysville Township, Pawnee County, near the small town of Rozel. Historically, the Brodbecks were merchants not farmers, so they were ill-equipped for this westward adventure.

The first year in Kansas the family lived in a sod house which was assembled from brick-shaped pieces of turf cut from the prairie, then stacked to form walls for a dwelling. This was a huge change for people used to living in houses made of wood and brick.

The soil of western Kansas was hard packed in those days, and it was a long and difficult task breaking up the prairie sod with just a horse and plow. In addition, the farmland the Brodbecks had received for homesteading was poor and rainfall was scarce. The one hundredth meridian designates a dividing line between adequate moisture and dry land farming conditions. Unfortunately, the Brodbecks were close to that divide.

A chance trip to Larned, the county seat, provided Charles with an opportunity to change his life as a farmer. He was intrigued by a small steam-powered Merry-Go-Round owned by the local blacksmith, and eventually talked the man into selling it to him in exchange for some land that had been part of the Oklahoma land rush.

Our family was now in the carnival business.

It was a small Merry-Go-Round, and maybe had sixteen horses. Charles began traveling around western Kansas, visiting local fairs and celebrations, carting the Merry-Go-Round with him on a wagon drawn by horses. He would assemble his Merry-Go-Round near a fairground and invite local residents to ride for five cents.

It wasn't long before Charles discovered he could make more money as a carnie than as a farmer.

Figure 2: Fred, Ben, Charles, Gene, and Josephine Brodbeck

During the next few years, each of Charles' sons, Fred, (b. 1880) Gene, (b. 1883) and Ben (b. 1890) developed their own shows, acquiring additional rides. Fred and Ben began traveling together so they could share expenses and have a bigger show.

In 1909, the brothers bought a Ferris Wheel from the Eli Bridge Company of Jacksonville, Illinois. Fred and Ben began scheduling dates to play in various communities.

As a carnie family, we were on our way.

My grandparents, Ben and Ruth, were married in 1910. She was nineteen years old. (b. 1891) I have often wondered what possessed her to marry a man who ran a carnival, which meant traveling around during the hottest months of the year and living in a tent.

Figure 3: The carnival midway

In the early years my family traveled from town to town in a railroad boxcar. Occasionally, we stayed in a community that had a small hotel. Many of the locations we played were so small that they lacked any overnight facilities. A hotel must have been a real treat for my grandmother. I didn't mind camping out as a kid.

At first, Ben operated the carousel while Ruth was in charge of the cookhouse. This structure was a wooden frame of counters and benches, covered with canvas, with a grill in the center. The patrons sat around the exterior. Her job was to feed all the people associated with the carnival so they could stay near the midway.

Later, she cooked for the public. Hamburgers and hot dogs were the main items on the menu. For many years, the cookhouse was an integral part of the carnival. As communities began to establish restaurants, and the Great Depression started, this aspect of the show faded.

Figure 4: Last teardown of the season: Duncan, Oklahoma, October 20, 1913

After the cookhouse closed, my grandmother sold tickets for the Merry-Go-Round. The tickets cost five cents each or ten for fifty cents. From her vantage point in the elevated ticket box, she ran the show with a firm hand. She had the final say and was demanding about each person's job performance.

We usually opened in the late afternoon, between 3 PM and 5 PM, the exact time depending on the day of the week. Sometimes Saturdays began as early as 10 AM. Rides had to be wiped clean, canvas sides raised, and ticket boxes staffed. Each ride had its own ticket box. Change was distributed. At the appointed time, Ruth looked around and raised her index finger, the official signal to open the show. The calliope music on the Merry-Go-Round would start to play, and we were in business for the day.

Figure 5: The author and her aunt Bernice

Figure 6: The Brodbeck boys: Buford, Melburn (dad), Ernest, & Ermil

Ben and Ruth raised five children, one girl and five boys were born to the couple. Bernice, the oldest, was born in 1914. My dad, Melburn, arrived in 1915. Maurice came along in 1918.

He died in a home laundry accident at two years of age. On a train trip to Florida in 1922, my Grandmother had to disembark the train in Griffith, Georgia, to deliver the twins, Ernest and Ermil. She didn't believe in doctors, so I am sure she had never consulted a physician. With a multiple birth, the babies probably came early.

The extended Brodbecks, Charles and his sons, their wives and assorted grandchildren wintered in Florida. After all, that's what carnival and circus people did in the 1920s. My uncle Buford was born in 1925, rounding out the family.

Figure 7: The Florida home

Our carnival was a family show, run by a family, for families. There were no inappropriate joints or "girly shows." My grandparents were straight laced and conservative. They didn't allow anything off-color.

Each April, a Brodbeck family representative journeyed to Topeka, the capitol of Kansas, to meet with the State Fair Board. This organization was a clearing house where carnivals and county fairs could match dates.

Figure 8: Ruth fishing in Florida

Since our carnival had the reputation as a clean family show, many towns wanted us to return year after year. Our family became friends with many civic leaders across the state. This rapport lent some continuity to our lives. It was great as a kid to return to my favorite places. One town might have an ice cream parlor, and another community might have a terrific swimming hole. Primarily, our carnival participated in celebrations and county fairs in western Kansas and western Oklahoma. We also went to two towns in Nebraska.

With their growing family, my grandparents needed to make better sleeping arrangements. Until the 1920s, the family slept in tents.

About that time, Ben built a plywood box on a single axle from an old pickup truck. Each side of the box had two fold down bunks. This contraption resembled an early form of a camping trailer.

Because this was their only secure structure, the family hid their cash in the camper. On one of their journeys, the trailer was involved in a traffic accident. A car knocked the trailer onto its side. The door flew open, and money scattered all over the highway. It took many people and several hours to pick up all the pennies, nickels, dimes, quarters, and half dollars lying all over the roadway.

My grandparents were never ones to trust banks so their money was never deposited in any account anywhere. Plus, in those days, banks were local establishments not even statewide. There were no such things as ATMs. In addition, running a carnival was a cash business, and for our family. It was fairly profitable.

As each member of the Brodbeck family matured, they became responsible for one aspect of the carnival.

Bernice and her husband, Dean, operated the Penny Pitch. This joint was a wooden two-by-four structure with canvas sides and top about twelve feet square. Patrons stood around the outside edge and threw pennies (later nickels, then dimes) at a low four-by-four platform containing Depression glass. If the money landed in the glassware, the customer won that dish as a prize.

Bernice and Dean also ran the Ball Throw. It was a long rectangular, wooden two-by-four structure with a waist high counter. A customer threw baseballs toward a target. Depending on how many stuffed shapes they knocked over, the player won a prize.

Finally, Dean ran the High-Striker (a strong man machine). The premise of this joint was to hit the metal striker with a rubber mallet and chime the bell at the top of the backboard.

Figure 9: The Hi-Striker Game

My parents, Melburn and Mary, (always know as "Bill") ran the Bingo game. It was another wooden, two-by-four frame joint with a canvas top. The structure was about twelve feet by twenty-four feet. In the center were two horseshoe-shaped shelf units which displayed prizes.

My dad sat at one end and called Bingo numbers. My mother sold Bingo cards for ten cents and gave each customer a supply of corn to mark their numbers.

At bedtime I curled up on two old trunks in the center of the Bingo joint, with my Indian style blanket that my son still has today. I fell asleep listening to my Dad say, "Under the G-68".

I would generally wake up the next morning in my own bed, a fold down sofa with a crease in the center. (I thought all good beds had a groove where your body could snuggle into.) Obviously, my dad had carried his sleeping daughter home from the Bingo joint to our trailer.

The twins, Ernest and Ermil, operated the tilt-a-whirl. This ride was a large shell-shaped capsule which went around a circular track with an up and down motion, all the while twirling the customer around and around. Their wives Deloris and Eileen sold tickets for them.

Buford ran the Ferris Wheel and his wife, Vera, sold tickets for him.

In addition, we had two kiddie rides. One was a small Ferris Wheel about twelve feet high, and the other was a circular kiddie-car ride. Sometimes we hired a local teenager to operate these two rides for us.

Figure 10: The Tilt-A-Whirl. Front: Ruth, Ben. Back: Mel, Ermil, and Buford

Over the years different families traveled with us. My favorite tag-a-longs were Jerome and Josephine Hadley from Tahlequah, Oklahoma. They had a self contained trailer which housed popcorn, snow cone, and cotton candy machines. Because I was a carnie kid, I could buy a treat for five cents. My mother gave me ten cents each night for treats. The general public had to pay a quarter for these goodies.

Another group of people who traveled with us owned Shetland ponies. It was so much fun to ride a real horse instead of a wooden one. Their daughter's name was Terry like mine. She became Little Terry, and I was known as Big Terry.

11: Ermil, Eileen, Buford, Vera, Mel, Mary, Deloris, Ernest

Our pack of kids was unique. Most of the time I was the oldest child; I was born in 1941. My cousin Leland came along in 1942. Cousin Linda arrived in 1943. By then all the Brodbeck brothers were serving in the Armed Forces. My Dad was in Europe with the Eighth Infantry Division, Ernest was in the Navy in the Aleutian Islands, Ermil was also in the Navy in the Philippines, and Buford was stationed in Texas.

During these war years Ruth's brothers, Harry and Ted (my great uncles) joined our carnival family. Ted brought along his kids, Kenny, Gladys, and Ruthie, who was my age. Harry ran the Ferris Wheel and Ted took over operation of the Merry-Go-Round. Kenny helped operated the kiddie rides. Discipline crossed family lines. If an adult told you to do something, or not to do something, you obeyed.

Figure 12: Terry, Linda, Leland

When I was four years old, my grandmother began training me to sell tickets. I would sit on her lap in the Merry-Go-Round ticket box. When a customer came up, laid their money on the counter, I would tear off the required number of tickets from the roll. Grandma would whisper in my ear the change to give the patron, though I quickly learned to figure it out in my head as well.

In 1955, when I was in the eighth grade and my family no longer traveled with the show, I visited my grandmother's carnival at the Sedgwick County Fair in Cheney, Kansas. I sold tickets for her that week. It was an eerie return to my roots. Even today, I find making change an automatic activity.

Almost every day our group of kids played cowboys and Indians on the Merry-Go-Round. We had a rule among ourselves that however old you were that year, you rode the horse with the corresponding number. It saved us a lot of arguing about who got to ride which horse. Each year we would move up to the next horse, sometimes losing our favorite horse to a cousin.

Figure 13: Lola, Ruth, Ted, Ines, and Harry

As I think back, it must have been hot in the middle of the summer with the canvas sides down. As kids, we had great fun. The heat must have really mattered to the adults, though. During the afternoons, the adults visited in the shade of the Merry-Go-Round. We had an early supper, but the wives seldom cooked. As a family, we generally went out to a local restaurant. Everyone was always so thrilled if the symbol of a penguin was on the front door. This meant that the building was air conditioned, a real treat in the 1940s.

Figure 14: Terry and Grandma Ruth, 1947

We often played school. Kenny was the teacher because he was the oldest by five years. Someone had nailed several old-time school desks onto a four by four. This contraption was off-loaded into a shady spot and kept all of us busy for the duration.

All of us kids loved Kingfisher, Oklahoma. We were first introduced to television in 1950 when I was nine years old in this city. Our carnival parked in a field next to the town limits. Right next to our trailers lived a family that had a TV set. In the evening, we would take lawn chairs and blankets over to their side yard. The family turned the television out toward the window. Little did I know how much this new invention would change our lives.

Figure 15: Grandma's school

We always played the celebration at Prague, Oklahoma, on the Fourth of July. This town really put on a great display of fireworks. Around 10 PM the midway would close and everyone congregated in a nearby field to watch the fireworks.

There was another town that we kids loved. I wish I could remember the name of it because I would love to go back and take my own children and grandchildren. Near our parking spot was a gravel bottomed stream. The water was clear with a three foot high waterfall. We would slide over the falls into a pool of water below. This early version of a water park kept us busy all day, or as long as a parent wanted to lifeguard.

If our destinations were always different, our weekly schedule was the same after we arrived in a new town.

Mondays were planning days for the men. The new midway would be organized. Sometimes the joints were assembled. The women gathered the children and the dirty clothes and headed to the local Laundromat. We always had fun because it was a new place to play.

Tuesday was set-up day: The rides were assembled and electrical cables were run to each attraction.

Wednesday, Thursday, Friday, and Saturday were our days for business. Saturday night after closing was for tearing down and loading all the parts onto trucks. Sometimes the guys worked from 10 AM until 2 AM getting things ready for Sunday. We were never open for business on Sunday because Blue Laws prohibited commerce on a Church Day.

We always got up early on Sunday mornings. It felt so strange to walk outside and see the vacant midway. The rides were loaded. The cables packed. The grass was beaten down in paths where customers had walked. A few torn tickets littered the ground. I always felt like the midway looked naked. Soon the caravan formed, and we were our way to our next destination.

My Dad always drove the first truck, after all he was the oldest son. His vehicle was a red Ford flatbed loaded with spare parts for the Merry-Go-Round. Next, came a large van loaded with the Merry-Go-Round horses. The Ferris Wheel, Tilt-a-Whirl, and Hot Wagon followed. The Hot Wagon contained a large portable generator inside a Chevy van. This purchase provided us with electricity after we arrived at our new destination.

Following the ride trucks were smaller trucks loaded with the joint parts. Last came the wives with their trailers. Each family member owned a travel trailer which the women pulled behind their personal vehicles. It must have been a nightmare for other travelers to come upon this caravan of several cars with trailers and about ten trucks filled with carnival parts.

Probably the fastest we traveled was forty miles-per-hour on old two-lane roadways that might only be dirt. There was no way to get past all of us on the road. When we reached our destination, the men parked the trailers, usually near some trees for shade. During the afternoon, the adults visited or napped while the kids explored our new surroundings. Because the Hot Wagon wasn't hooked up to city electricity until Monday, we went to bed Sunday night with coal oil lanterns providing illumination.

Each year the carnival traveled from April to October. The kids began to assemble after school was out in the spring. We went home to Kinsley, Kansas, late in August. As we arrived at new towns, we would set up the midway either on a downtown street or in a field near the fairgrounds. Each week was a new adventure. When we parked near a fairground, with the county fair in progress, there were numerous farm animals to see, quilts to observe, food to eat, and rodeos to attend. I never really got into the horse scene as many young girls do. I was content to ride the wooden variety of horse with a pole in its center that went up and down to calliope music.

One of our biggest fears for the carnival was the unpredictability of the weather. Kansas and Oklahoma have several tornados each year. Some nights when the wind was fierce, the men would unload the cars on the Ferris Wheel. Next, they tied four to six ropes on each side of the ride. The men would hang on to the ropes to keep the wheel from blowing over. Those of us in the trailers just had to take our chances.

I usually slept until 10 AM. I had breakfast in our trailer, then went outside for my bath. My mother filled a galvanized tub with water early in the morning. She let the water warm by solar power. Dressed in my bathing suit, I scrubbed myself then put on clean clothes, I was ready for a day of adventure.

My first experience of sexual discrimination also occurred on the carnival. My Grandmother allowed my cousin Leland to jump off of or onto the moving Merry-Go-Round because he was a boy. She wouldn't let me because I was a girl. I might get hurt. I was probably about seven at the time. My cousin Ruthie told me that she used to jump on and off. She just went on the other side of the Merry-Go-Round so her Aunt Ruth couldn't see what she was doing. I never thought of solving the problem in this manner.

Ben owned a cement block building behind the Main Street Café in Kinsley, Kansas. The family used this facility for repairs on the carnival equipment. In the fall, one by one each truck was unloaded. All the parts were inspected. Any repairs were made. Items were painted. Finally, the trucks were reloaded and transported to a warehouse behind Ben and Ruth's house on Third Street. When I didn't have school, my Dad would take me along to help. With a board, a can of paint and a brush I pretended to work.

Figure 16: Benjamin Harrison Brodbeck

During the 1940s, Ben's health began to deteriorate. He was diagnosed with ascending creeping paralysis, possibly Lou Gehrig's Disease. He was confined to a wheel chair in 1943. He still participated in carnival life. Near the end, Leland, Linda and I were ushered into the big back bedroom of their house in Kinsley. This was probably our opportunity to see our Grandfather for the last time. I don't know if he was still alive then or not. He died on February 6, 1945, before any of his boys came home from the service. Family members believe that having his sons so far away contributed to his death.

After the brothers returned form the service, Buford and my Dad decided we needed a more thrilling ride. The brothers each obtained a G. I. loan for $4500 and they bought a Spit Fire. This ride had a circular frame with airplanes. It sat at a forty-five degree angle. As the ride moved forward, the planes rotated on the axis. The brothers saved all the profit from the ride, paying off the loan in four years. Of course this ride gave Kenny a way to torment the girls. If we got in an airplane to have an overseas adventure, he would hook the door and spin us around.

The end of World War II altered carnival life.

First, all of the boys came home. We were very lucky, but the whole culture of American life changed. The Brodbeck brothers had seen the world. While they could hardly wait to get home, their horizons had expanded.

Educational opportunities became available for veterans. Women were now a part of the work force. People began to take real vacations. Television became a part of daily life. No longer was the once a year visit by the carnival the only entertainment for a community. Soon, individual towns built their own amusement parks.

Slowly, business began to fall off. One by one, the brothers left the show.

Ernest was the first to leave in 1947. He went to work at a furniture store in Great Bend, Kansas.

Buford bought a cleaning establishment in Kinsley in 1948.

Ermil moved to Hutchinson, Kansas, in 1949 and worked at a wholesale plumbing firm, Western Supply, Inc.

My dad was the next to leave. He joined Ermil and worked at the Wichita branch of the same firm. We moved to the big city of Wichita in 1951. I was devastated to give up my life as a carnie.

Bernice and Dean stayed with my Grandmother until 1955 when they bought a liquor store in Kinsley.

Ted continued to travel with the show until Ruth sold the Merry-Go-Round and Ferris Wheel to Mr. Randall of Liberal, Kansas, in the 1960s. She moved her trailer to western Kansas and sold tickets for him for years.

I never remember being rich or poor as a kid. My Uncle Buford said that the goal of the carnival was to make $50 per ride each day that we were open. This amount kept each family solvent for the year. He told me about some celebrations that brought in $1,200 per day. At one town the rides grossed $3,000 for one day. This was the 1940s and 1950s when an annual income of $3,000 per year was considered middle class. Our family never had any liability insurance. Over the years only two patrons had minor injuries. We were very lucky.

I was a carnie kid until I was ten years old, longer than any of the other cousins. For this reason I feel it is important to tell our story. It is a piece of Americana that is lost and won't be repeated. Later generations won't understand what it was like in America in those years. If I don't share my childhood, it may be gone. We had a great time. I think this early lifestyle influenced the kind of person that I am now. I still like to travel and explore new places. Curiosity is a part of my life.

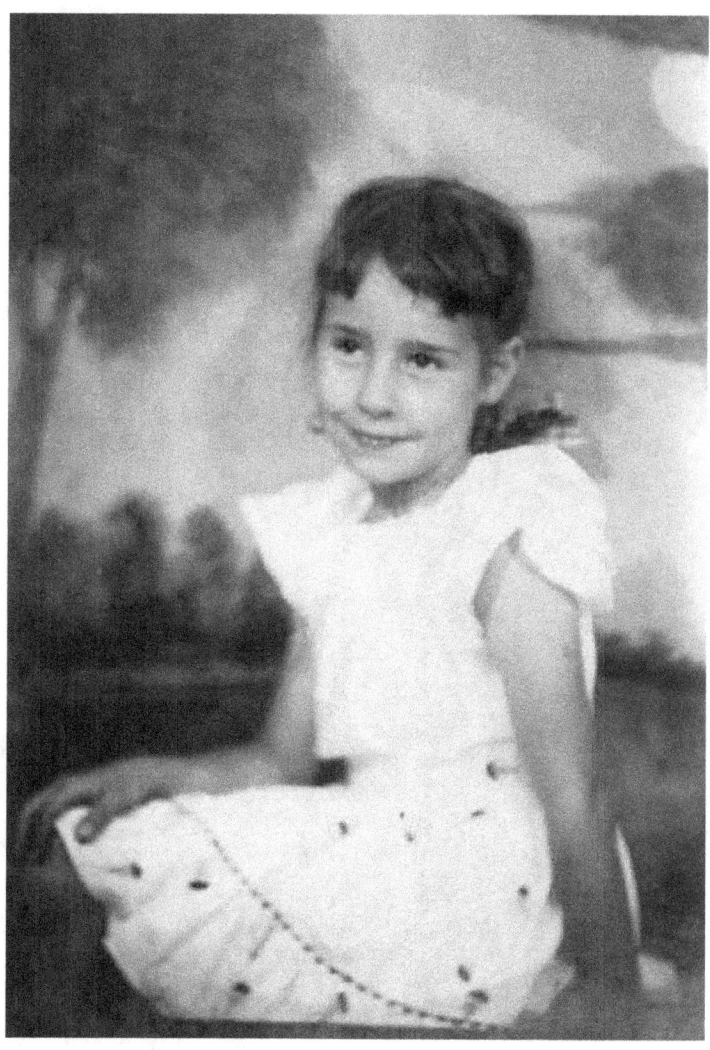

Figure 17: The Author in pigtails

About Knotted Road Press

Knotted Road Press fiction specializes in dynamic writing set in mysterious, exotic locations.

Knotted Road Press non-fiction publishes autobiographies, cookbooks, and how-to books with unique voices.

Knotted Road Press creates DRM-free ebooks as well as high-quality print books for readers around the world.

With authors in a variety of genres including literary, poetry, mystery, fantasy, and science fiction, Knotted Road Press has something for everyone.

Knotted Road Press
www.KnottedRoadPress.com

www.ingramcontent.com/pod-product-compliance
Lightning Source LLC
Chambersburg PA
CBHW072116290426
44110CB00014B/1932